THE CHRISTIAN LIFE PROFILE

ASSESSMENT WORKBOOK

Praise for
The Christian Life Profile Assessment Workbook

Randy Frazee is not only seriously concerned with knowing if Christians are actually growing and changing; he and his team have come up with a way to both measure and facilitate real spiritual growth. And he's depending on spiritual community to make it happen.

Larry Crabb Jr., author of *The Safest Place on Earth*

The Christian Life Profile project provides an assessment of where people are in terms of the two central dimensions of faith — love for God and love for neighbor. When these measurements are used in the context of others, in community, the findings can be enlightening, empowering, and liberating, leading to transformed lives. *The Christian Life Profile* assessment is the best of its kind.

George Gallup Jr., coauthor of *The Next American Spirituality*

The Christian Life Profile assessment and the program of discipleship focused around it is by far the best corporate plan for spiritual formation and spiritual growth that I know of in the corporate setting. It expresses the highest quality of Christian devotion, intelligence, and practical understanding of the dynamics of growth in Christ. Christian groups and leaders can be sure that resolute application of this in their context will progressively move their people toward realization of the goal Christ set before us: "teaching them to do all things I have commanded you." One would have to go all the way back to the "Band" groups of John Wesley to find anything that compares. Christ's plan for world revolution through the transformation of individuals and communities under his governance is still on his agenda. Adoption of this assessment can ensure that it is on ours as well.

Dallas Willard, author of *The Divine Conspiracy*

THE CHRISTIAN LIFE PROFILE

ASSESSMENT WORKBOOK

DEVELOPING YOUR PERSONAL PLAN TO THINK, ACT, and BE LIKE JESUS

PREVIOUSLY PUBLISHED AS
THE CHRISTIAN LIFE PROFILE ASSESSMENT TOOL WORKBOOK

RANDY FRAZEE

ZONDERVAN

The Christian Life Profile™ Assessment Workbook Updated Edition
Copyright © 1998, 2001, 2005 by Randy Frazee

Previously published as *The Christian Life Profile Assessment Tool Workbook.*

This title is also available as a Zondervan ebook. Visit www.zondervan.com/ebooks.

Requests for information should be addressed to:

Zondervan, 3900 *Sparks Dr. SE, Grand Rapids, Michigan 49546*

ISBN 978-0-310-88829-1

Cover design: Lucas Art and Design
Interior design: Dan Dingman

First Printing April 2015 / Printed in the United States of America

Contents

Concentrate on the four dots in the middle
of the picture for thirty-five seconds. Then
look at a white surface and keep looking
until the white circle disappears.

Foreword

George Gallup Jr.

The central challenge for Christians is embodied in Jesus Christ's Great Commandment from Luke 10:27: "'Love the Lord your God with all your heart and with all your soul and with all your strength and with all your mind'; and 'Love your neighbor as yourself.'"

Two key questions must be asked of Christians: "*How* are you following this Great Commandment?" and, "*To what degree* are you following this Great Commandment?" If church leaders are serious about building disciples, or followers, of Jesus Christ, they need to try to gain a sense of how people are answering these questions.

Randy Frazee has responded to this vital need by offering The Christian Life Profile assessment as a gift to churches. With encouragement from Bob Buford of Leadership Network, as well as through consultation with local and national religious leaders, a list of thirty statements was developed, divided between a "love of God" scale and a "love of neighbor" scale. Both love dimensions were examined on the basis of beliefs (what we need to *know*), practices (what we need to *do*), and Christian virtues (what we need to *be*, described by Frazee as "the ultimate expression of Christlikeness").

This assessment provides a way for individuals and congregations to become "fully developing disciples." The author stresses the point that such growth can best happen in biblically based gatherings or small groups.

And what are the fruits of the application of this assessment? The evidence is powerful—both for individual congregations and for society as a whole. In a nationwide Gallup Institute survey, it was discovered that those surveyed who have a deep love of God (based on the "love of God" scale) are far more likely than other Christians to say they agree with the statements "God calls me to be involved in the lives of the poor and suffering"; "I believe it is important to share the gospel faith with my neighbor because Christ has commanded me to do so"; "I pray for non-Christians to accept Jesus Christ as their Lord and Savior"; "I give away my time to serve and help others in my community"; and "My first priority in spending is to support God's work."

These (and the other items on the "love of God" scale) reveal a solid connection between a deep love for God and the way people lead their lives, underscoring the transforming power of The Christian Life Profile assessment and pointing to the huge societal impact that could result from the widespread application of this breakthrough instrument.

George Gallup Jr. (April 19, 1930 – November 21, 2011) was an American pollster, writer, and executive at the Gallup Organization.

Introduction

Life Is a Journey!

Do people see a profile of Jesus Christ when they observe your life? The apostle Paul wrote in Galatians 4:19 – 20, "My dear children, for whom I am again in the pains of childbirth until Christ is formed in you, how I wish I could be with you now." Paul's words speak to the primary mission of the church — to see a person establish an eternal relationship with Jesus Christ that grows and develops until Christ is seen in them. The Christian Life Profile assessment has been created to help you in that process.

But what specifically does a follower of Christ look like? What are the characteristics or marks that form a profile of Christ in us? The Christian Life Profile assessment is founded on the words of Jesus in Luke 10:27, where he suggests that the essential focus of the spiritual life boils down to loving God as the first priority and loving our neighbors as ourselves. Christian maturity is primarily about relationships: with God and with others.

What are the key ideas of someone who is increasingly growing in his or her love for God and for others? This assessment identifies thirty key ideas. These thirty are not exhaustive but are key characteristics we see over and over again in the Bible. Of the thirty, ten are key beliefs (*think* like Jesus). The second set of ten are key practices (*act* like Jesus). The final ten are key virtues (*be* like Jesus). Our beliefs and practices are meaningless until they transform us into people whose love is seen in these ten key virtues the Bible calls "the fruit of the Spirit." We have also added "hope" and "humility" to the list found in Galatians 5. We refer to these ten key beliefs, ten key practices, and ten key virtues as the thirty Key Ideas.

The statements to which you will be responding seek to assess how fully you have developed this Christlike profile. Keep in mind that this does not compare your level of spiritual maturity with someone else's. For example, if you scored a three in prayer and another person scored a five and another a one, it doesn't mean you have grown more or less in this practice than the others. This self-assessment only compares you to the model Christ set forth. It is designed to help you discover the areas where you are the strongest as well as the areas where you need to grow in your Christian life. The goal is for you to target a specific area you'd like to develop in your spiritual journey. As George Gallup Jr. said of this assessment, "It is not so much for spiritual measurement as it is to create spiritual movement."

The Christian Life Profile assessment is most effective when used in the context of biblical community, such as a small group. The members of the group provide support, encouragement, accountability, and prayer for each other as they individually and corporately seek to grow in Christ's likeness. The assessment even suggests you allow three other people to answer a set of questions about you to help you in your assessment. This is one of its most beneficial aspects.

Approach this process with great anticipation and openness to the wonderful life God has in store for you as you seek to grow in the grace and knowledge of our Lord Jesus Christ.

Architecture of the Assessment

Connections	Categories	(Key Ideas) Competencies
	Beliefs	1. God
		2. Personal God
		3. Salvation
		4. The Bible
		5. Identity in Christ
		6. Church
		7. Humanity
		8. Compassion
		9. Stewardship
		10. Eternity
LOVE GOD	Practices	1. Worship
		2. Prayer
		3. Bible Study
		4. Single-Mindedness
		5. Total Surrender
		6. Biblical Community
		7. Spiritual Gifts
		8. Offering My Time
		9. Giving My Resources
		10. Sharing My Faith
LOVE NEIGHBOR	Virtues	1. Love
		2. Joy
		3. Peace
		4. Self-Control
		5. Hope
		6. Patience
		7. Kindness/Goodness
		8. Faithfulness
		9. Gentleness
		10. Humility

DESCRIPTION OF THE 30 KEY IDEAS

Key Ideas: Beliefs

God

Key Idea: I believe the God of the Bible is the one true God — Father, Son, and Holy Spirit.

Key Verse: 2 Corinthians 13:14 "May the grace of the Lord Jesus Christ, and the love of God, and the fellowship of the Holy Spirit be with you all."

Assessment Statements:

1. I believe the God of the Bible is the only true God. (Q. #1)
2. I believe the God of the Bible is one in essence but distinct in person — Father, Son, and Holy Spirit (Q. #31).
3. I believe Jesus is God in the flesh — who died and rose bodily from the dead. (Q. #61)
4. I believe the Holy Spirit is God and dwells in Christians to empower them to live the Christian life. (Q. #91)

Personal God

Key Idea: I believe God is involved in and cares about my daily life.

Key Verse: Psalm 121:1 – 2 "I lift up my eyes to the mountains — where does my help come from? My help comes from the LORD, the Maker of heaven and earth."

Assessment Statements:

1. I believe God has a purpose for my life. (Q. #2)
2. I believe pain and suffering can often bring me closer to God. (Q. #32)
3. I believe God is actively involved in my life. (Q. #62)
4. I believe God enables me to do things I could not or would not otherwise do. (Q. #92)

Salvation

Key Idea: I believe a person comes into a right relationship with God, by his grace, through faith in Jesus Christ.

Key Verse: Ephesians 2:8 – 9 "For it is by grace you have been saved, through faith — and this is not from yourselves, it is the gift of God — not by works, so that no one can boast."

Assessment Statements:

1. I believe I will inherit eternal life because of what Jesus has done for me. (Q. #3)
2. I believe nothing I do or have done can earn my salvation. (Q. #33)
3. I believe salvation comes only through Jesus. (Q. #63)
4. I believe people are saved because of what Jesus did, not because of what they do. (Q. #93)

The Bible

Key Idea: I believe the Bible is the Word of God and has the right to command my belief and action.

Key Verse: 2 Timothy 3:16 – 17 "All Scripture is God-breathed and is useful for teaching, rebuking, correcting and training in righteousness, so that the servant of God may be thoroughly equipped for every good work."

Assessment Statements:

1. I believe the Bible is absolutely true in matters of faith and morals. (Q. #4)
2. I believe the words of the Bible are words from God. (Q. #34)
3. I believe the Bible has decisive authority over what I say and do. (Q. #64)
4. I believe the Bible is relevant to address the needs of contemporary culture. (Q. #94)

Identity in Christ

Key Idea: I am significant because of my position as a child of God.

Key Verse: John 1:12 "Yet to all who did receive him, to those who believed in his name, he gave the right to become children of God."

Assessment Statements:

1. I believe God loves me and therefore my life has value. (Q. #5)
2. I believe that I exist to know, love, and serve God. (Q. #35)
3. I believe God loves me, even when I do not obey him. (Q. #65)
4. I believe I am forgiven and accepted by God. (Q. #95)

Church

Key Idea: I believe the church is God's primary way to accomplish his purposes on earth today.

Key Verse: Ephesians 4:15 – 16 "Instead, speaking the truth in love, we will grow to become in every respect the mature body of him who is the head, that is, Christ. From him the whole body, joined and held together by every supporting ligament, grows and builds itself up in love, as each part does its work."

Assessment Statements:

1. I believe God gives spiritual gifts to every Christian for service to the church and the community. (Q. #6)

2. I believe I cannot grow as a Christian unless I am an active member of a local church. (Q. #36)

3. I believe the community of true believers is Christ's body on earth. (Q. #66)

4. I believe the purpose of the church is to share the gospel and nurture Christians to maturity in Christ. (Q. #96)

Humanity

Key Idea: I believe all people are loved by God and need Jesus Christ as their Savior.

Key Verse: John 3:16 "For God so loved the world that he gave his only Son, that whoever believes in him shall not perish but have eternal life."

Assessment Statements:

1. I believe each person possesses a sinful nature and is in need of God's forgiveness. (Q. #7)

2. I believe we are created in the image of God and therefore have equal value, regardless of race, religion, or gender. (Q. #37)

3. I believe all people are loved by God; therefore, I too should love them. (Q. #67)

4. I believe God desires all people to have a relationship with Jesus Christ. (Q. #97)

Compassion

Key Idea: I believe God calls all Christians to show compassion to those in need.

Key Verse: Psalm 82:3–4 "Defend the cause of the weak and fatherless; uphold the cause of the poor and the oppressed. Rescue the weak and needy; deliver them from the hand of the wicked."

Assessment Statements:

1. I believe that God calls me to be involved in the lives of the poor and suffering. (Q. #8)

2. I believe I am responsible before God to show compassion to the sick and imprisoned. (Q. #38)

3. I believe I should stand up for those who cannot stand up for themselves. (Q. #68)

4. I believe Christians should not purchase everything they can afford, so that their discretionary money might be available to help those in need. (Q. #98)

Stewardship

Key Idea: I believe everything I am or own belongs to God.

Key Verse: Psalm 24:1 "The earth is the LORD's, and everything in it, the world, and all who live in it."

Assessment Statements:

1. I believe everything I am or own comes from God and belongs to God. (Q. #9)

2. I believe a Christian should live a sacrificial life, not driven by pursuit of material things. (Q. #39)

3. I believe that Christians should give at least 10 percent of their income to God's work. (Q. #69)

4. I believe God will bless Christians now and in the life to come for their good works. (Q. #99)

Eternity

Key Idea: I believe there is a heaven and a hell and that Jesus will return to judge all people and to establish his eternal kingdom.

Key Verse: John 14:1–2 "Do not let your hearts be troubled. You believe in God; believe also in me. My Father's house has many rooms; if that were not so, would I have told you that I am going there to prepare a place for you?"

Assessment Statements:

1. I believe it is important to share the gospel with my neighbor because Christ has commanded me to do so. (Q. #10)

2. I believe that people who deliberately reject Jesus Christ as Savior will not inherit eternal life. (Q. #40)

3. I believe that every person is subject to the judgment of God. (Q. #70)

4. I believe all people who place their trust in Jesus Christ will spend eternity in heaven. (Q. #100)

Key Ideas: Practices

Worship

Key Idea: I worship God for who he is and what he has done for me.

Key Verse: Psalm 95:1 – 2 "Come, let us sing for joy to the LORD; let us shout aloud to the Rock of our salvation. Let us come before him with thanksgiving and extol him with music and song."

Assessment Statements:

1. I thank God daily for who he is and what he is doing in my life. (Q. #11)
2. I attend religious services and worship with other believers each week. (Q. #41)
3. I give God the credit for all that I am and all that I possess. (Q. #71)
4. I am not ashamed for others to know that I worship God. (Q. #101)

Prayer

Key Idea: I pray to God to know him, to find direction for my life, and to lay my requests before him.

Key Verse: Psalm 66:18 – 20 "If I had cherished sin in my heart, the Lord would not have listened; but God has surely listened and has heard my prayer. Praise be to God, who has not rejected my prayer or withheld his love from me!"

Assessment Statements:

1. I seek God's will through prayer. (Q. #12)
2. I regularly confess my sins to God. (Q. #42)
3. Prayer is a central part of my daily life. (Q. #72)
4. I seek to grow closer to God by listening to him in prayer. (Q. #102)

Bible Study

Key Idea: I study the Bible to know God and his truth and to find direction for my daily life.

Key Verse: Hebrews 4:12 "For the word of God is alive and active. Sharper than any double-edged sword, it penetrates even to dividing soul and spirit, joints and marrow; it judges the thoughts and attitudes of the heart."

Assessment Statements:

1. I read the Bible daily. (Q. #13)
2. I regularly study the Bible to find direction for my life. (Q. #43)
3. I seek to be obedient to God by applying the truth of the Bible to my life. (Q. #73)
4. I have a good understanding of the contents of the Bible. (Q. #103)

Single-Mindedness

Key Idea: I focus on God and his priorities for my life.

Key Verse: Matthew 6:33 "But seek first his kingdom and his righteousness, and all these things will be given to you as well."

Assessment Statements:

1. I desire Jesus Christ to be first in my life. (Q. #14)
2. I see every aspect of my life and work as service to God. (Q. #44)
3. I spend time each day reading God's Word and praying. (Q. #74)
4. I value a simple lifestyle over one cluttered with activities and material possessions. (Q. #104)

Total Surrender

Key Idea: I dedicate my life to God's purposes.

Key Verse: Romans 12:1 "Therefore, I urge you, brothers and sisters, in view of God's mercy, to offer your bodies as a living sacrifice, holy and pleasing to God — this is your true and proper worship."

Assessment Statements:

1. I am living out God's purposes for my life. (Q. #15)
2. I give up what I want to meet the needs of others. (Q. #45)
3. I give away things I possess when I am so led by God. (Q. #75)
4. I serve God through my daily work. (Q. #105)

Biblical Community

Key Idea: I fellowship with Christians to accomplish God's purposes in my life, in the lives of others, and in the world.

Key Ideas: Practices

Key Verse: Acts 2:44–47 "All the believers were together and had everything in common. They sold property and possessions to give to anyone who had need. Every day they continued to meet together in the temple courts. They broke bread in their homes and ate together with glad and sincere hearts, praising God and enjoying the favor of all the people. And the Lord added to their number daily those who were being saved."

Assessment Statements:

1. I have close relationships with other Christians who have influence on my life's direction. (Q. #16)
2. I participate in a group of Christians who really know me and support me. (Q. #46)
3. I allow other Christians to hold me accountable for my actions. (Q. #76)
4. I daily pray for and support other Christians. (Q. #106)

Spiritual Gifts

Key Idea: I know my spiritual gifts and use them to fulfill God's purposes.

Key Verse: Romans 12:4–6 "For just as each of us has one body with many members, and these members do not all have the same function, so in Christ we, though many, form one body, and each member belongs to all the others. We have different gifts, according to the grace given to each of us."

Assessment Statements:

1. I know my spiritual gift(s). (Q. #17)
2. I regularly use my spiritual gift(s) in ministry to accomplish God's purposes. (Q. #47)
3. I value the spiritual gifts of others to accomplish God's purposes. (Q. #77)
4. Others recognize and affirm my spiritual gift(s) and support my use of them. (Q. #107)

Offering My Time

Key Idea: I offer my time to fulfill God's purposes.

Key Verse: Colossians 3:17 "And whatever you do, whether in word or deed, do it all in the name of the Lord Jesus, giving thanks to God the Father through him."

Assessment Statements:

1. I invest my time in others by praying for them. (Q. #18)
2. I spend a good deal of time helping people with physical, emotional, or other kinds of needs. (Q. #48)
3. I give away my time to serve and help others in my community. (Q. #78)
4. I regularly volunteer at my church. (Q. #108)

Giving My Resources

Key Idea: I give away my resources to serve God and others.

Key Verse: 2 Corinthians 8:7 "But since you excel in everything—in faith, in speech, in knowledge, in complete earnestness and in the love we have kindled in you—see that you also excel in this grace of giving."

Assessment Statements:

1. I give away 10 percent or more of my income to God's work. (Q. #19)
2. I regularly give money to serve and help others. (Q. #49)
3. My first priority in spending is to support God's work. (Q. #79)
4. My spending habits do not keep me from giving what I feel I should give to God. (Q. #109)

Sharing My Faith

Key Idea: I share my faith with others to fulfill God's purposes.

Key Verse: Ephesians 6:19–20 "Pray also for me, that whenever I speak, words may be given me so that I will fearlessly make known the mystery of the gospel, for which I am an ambassador in chains. Pray that I may declare it fearlessly, as I should."

Assessment Statements:

1. I frequently share my faith with people who are not Christians. (Q. #20)
2. I try to live so that others will see Christ in my life. (Q. #50)
3. I know how to share my faith with non-Christians. (Q. #80)
4. I pray for non-Christians to accept Jesus Christ as their Lord and Savior. (Q. #110)

Key Ideas: Virtues

Love

Key Idea: I am committed to loving God and loving others.

Key Verse: 1 John 4:10 – 12 "This is love: not that we loved God, but that he loved us and sent his Son as an atoning sacrifice for our sins. Dear friends, since God so loved us, we also ought to love one another. No one has ever seen God; but if we love one another, God lives in us and his love is made complete in us."

Assessment Statements:

1. God's grace enables me to forgive people who have hurt me. (Q. #21)
2. I rejoice when good things happen to other people. (Q. #51)
3. I demonstrate love equally toward people of all races. (Q. #81)
4. I frequently give up what I want for the sake of others. (Q. #111)

Joy

Key Idea: Despite my circumstances, I feel inner contentment and understand my purpose in life.

Key Verse: John 15:11 "I have told you this so that my joy may be in you and that your joy may be complete."

Assessment Statements:

1. I have inner contentment even when things go wrong. (Q. #22)
2. Circumstances do not dictate my mood. (Q. #52)
3. I am excited about the sense of purpose I have for my life. (Q. #82)
4. I can be content with the money and possessions I now have. (Q. #112)

Peace

Key Idea: I am free from anxiety because things are right between God, others, and myself.

Key Verse: Philippians 4:6 – 7 "Do not be anxious about anything, but in every situation, by prayer and petition, with thanksgiving, present your requests to God. And the peace of God, which transcends all understanding, will guard your hearts and your minds in Christ Jesus."

Assessment Statements:

1. I know God has forgiven me because of what Jesus has done. (Q. #23)
2. I am not angry with God, myself, or others. (Q. #53)
3. I forgive people who deeply hurt me. (Q. #83)
4. I have an inner peace from God. (Q. #113)

Self-Control

Key Idea: I have the power, through Christ, to control myself.

Key Scripture: Titus 2:11 – 13 "For the grace of God has appeared that offers salvation to all people. It teaches us to say 'No' to ungodliness and worldly passions, and to live self-controlled, upright and godly lives in this present age, while we wait for the blessed hope — the appearing of the glory of our great God and Savior, Jesus Christ."

Assessment Statements:

1. I am not addicted to any substances — whether food, caffeine, tobacco, alcohol, or chemical. (Q. #24)
2. I do not burst in anger out toward others. (Q. #54)
3. I do not have sexual relationships that are contrary to biblical teaching. (Q. #84)
4. I control my tongue. (Q. #114)

Hope

Key Idea: I can cope with the hardships of life and death because of the hope I have in Jesus Christ.

Key Verse: Hebrews 6:19 – 20 "We have this hope as an anchor for the soul, firm and secure. It enters the inner sanctuary behind the curtain, where our forerunner, Jesus, has entered on our behalf."

Assessment Statements:

1. I think a great deal about heaven and what God is preparing for me as a Christian. (Q. #25)
2. I am confident that God is working everything out for my good, regardless of the circumstances today. (Q. #55)
3. My hope in God increases through my daily pursuit to live like Christ. (Q. #85)
4. My hope for the future is not found in my health or wealth because both are so uncertain, but in God. (Q. #115)

Key Ideas: Virtues

Patience

Key Idea: I am slow to anger and endure patiently under the unavoidable pressures of life.

Key Verse: Proverbs 14:29 "Whoever is patient has great understanding, but one who is quick-tempered displays folly."

Assessment Statements:

1. I do not get angry with God when I have to endure suffering. (Q. #26)
2. I am known to maintain honesty and integrity when under pressure. (Q. #56)
3. I always put matters into God's hands when I am under pressure. (Q. #86)
4. I keep my composure even when people or circumstances irritate me. (Q. #116)

Kindness/Goodness

Key Idea: I choose to be kind and good in my relationships with others.

Key Verse: 1 Thessalonians 5:15 "Make sure that nobody pays back wrong for wrong, but always strive to do what is good for each other and for everyone else."

Assessment Statements:

1. I would never keep money that didn't belong to me. (Q. #27)
2. I am known as a person who speaks words of kindness to those in need of encouragement. (Q. #57)
3. I give to others expecting nothing in return. (Q. #87)
4. I help those who are in trouble or who cannot help themselves. (Q. #117)

Faithfulness

Key Idea: I have established a good name with God and others based on my loyalty to those relationships.

Key Verse: Proverbs 3:3–4 "Let love and faithfulness never leave you; bind them around your neck, write them on the tablet of your heart. Then you will win favor and a good name in the sight of God and man."

Assessment Statements:

1. I take unpopular stands when my faith dictates. (Q. #28)
2. I discipline my thoughts based on my faith in Jesus Christ. (Q. #58)
3. I follow God even when it involves suffering. (Q. #88)
4. I follow through on commitments I have made to God. (Q. #118)

Gentleness

Key Idea: I am thoughtful, considerate, and calm in my dealings with others.

Key Verse: Philippians 4:5 "Let your gentleness be evident to all. The Lord is near."

Assessment Statements:

1. I consider my own shortcomings when faced with the failures of others. (Q. #29)
2. I am known as a person who is sensitive to the needs of others. (Q. #59)
3. I am known for not raising my voice. (Q. #89)
4. I allow people to make mistakes. (Q. #119)

Humility

Key Idea: I choose to esteem others above myself.

Key Verse: Philippians 2:3–4 "Do nothing out of selfish ambition or vain conceit. Rather, in humility value others above yourselves, not looking to your own interests but each of you to the interests of the others."

Assessment Statements:

1. As a child of God, I do not think too highly or too lowly of myself. (Q. #30)
2. I am not known as a person who brags. (Q. #60)
3. I am willing to make any of my faults known to Christians who care for me. (Q. #90)
4. I am not upset when my achievements are not recognized. (Q. #120)

PERSONAL ASSESSMENT

Getting Started

Begin with Prayer

Life change is an impossible task without God working in our lives. Thankfully, for our sakes, the Bible presents life transformation as a foregone conclusion in the scope of God's desire for us. Each of us needs to realize the importance of allowing God to be the initiator of our spiritual transformation. We need to begin this assessment process by presenting ourselves as humbly dependent on him. Ask God to help you see your life clearly as you respond to each statement. Recognize that it is the Holy Spirit within the Christian who enables him or her to grow spiritually.

Assessing Your Life

The following 120 statements relate to the key beliefs, practices, and virtues of the developing disciple. Read each statement, then assess your own personal Christian experience on a scale from 0 (Does not apply at all) to 5 (Applies completely).

Here are a couple of tips that will help you better assess yourself and therefore create more effective results.

1. When you come to a statement you don't understand, mark yourself low.

2. When you come to a statement on belief, don't score yourself on whether you believe it is the right answer but rather on whether it is a way of life for you. (For example, "I believe God is actively involved in my life." You may believe this is the right answer, but you don't sense he's actually involved in your life today. If this is the case, score yourself low.)

Instructions

1. The first step is to go to the "One Another" assessments section (page 35). You'll want to pass these pages out as soon as possible so you can complete the total assessment in a timely manner. Read and follow the instructions found on page 36.

2. Take the assessment starting on the next page. Circle your responses to the 120 statements in the corresponding numbered space to the right.

3. When you have completed the assessment, you will be guided through the measurement process to determine your results on page 32.

4. When you have completed the measurement step of the program, you will tabulate the responses of your "One Another" assessments (page 43). Reread the instructions on page 36 for assistance in completing this step.

5. You are now ready to develop a personal plan for spiritual growth (pages 46 – 49).

Ready to grow? Let's go!

Personal Assessment

	Does not apply at all		Applies somewhat		Applies completely
	0 1	2	3	4	5

1. I believe the God of the Bible is the only true God. — 0 1 2 3 4 5

2. I believe God has a purpose for my life. — 0 1 2 3 4 5

3. I believe I will inherit eternal life because of what Jesus has done for me. — 0 1 2 3 4 5

4. I believe the Bible is absolutely true in matters of faith and morals. — 0 1 2 3 4 5

5. I believe God loves me and therefore my life has value. — 0 1 2 3 4 5

6. I believe God gives spiritual gifts to every Christian for service to the church and the community. — 0 1 2 3 4 5

7. I believe each person possesses a sinful nature and is in need of God's forgiveness. — 0 1 2 3 4 5

8. I believe that God calls me to be involved in the lives of the poor and suffering. — 0 1 2 3 4 5

9. I believe everything I am or own comes from God and belongs to God. — 0 1 2 3 4 5

10. I believe it is important to share the gospel with my neighbor because Christ has commanded me to do so. — 0 1 2 3 4 5

11. I thank God daily for who he is and what he is doing in my life. — 0 1 2 3 4 5

12. I seek God's will through prayer. — 0 1 2 3 4 5

13. I read the Bible daily. — 0 1 2 3 4 5

14. I desire Jesus Christ to be first in my life. — 0 1 2 3 4 5

15. I am living out God's purposes for my life. — 0 1 2 3 4 5

16. I have close relationships with other Christians who have influence on my life's direction. — 0 1 2 3 4 5

17. I know my spiritual gifts. — 0 1 2 3 4 5

Personal Assessment

	Does not apply at all		Applies somewhat		Applies completely

18. I invest my time in others by praying for them. — 0 1 2 3 4 5

19. I give away 10 percent or more of my income to God's work. — 0 1 2 3 4 5

20. I frequently share my faith with people who are not Christians. — 0 1 2 3 4 5

21. God's grace enables me to forgive people who have hurt me. — 0 1 2 3 4 5

22. I have inner contentment even when things go wrong. — 0 1 2 3 4 5

23. I know God has forgiven me because of what Jesus has done. — 0 1 2 3 4 5

24. I am not addicted to any substances — whether food, caffeine, tobacco, alcohol, or chemical. — 0 1 2 3 4 5

25. I think a great deal about heaven and what God is preparing for me as a Christian. — 0 1 2 3 4 5

26. I do not get angry with God when I have to endure suffering. — 0 1 2 3 4 5

27. I would never keep money that didn't belong to me. — 0 1 2 3 4 5

28. I take unpopular stands when my faith dictates. — 0 1 2 3 4 5

29. I consider my own shortcomings when faced with the failures of others. — 0 1 2 3 4 5

30. As a child of God, I do not think too highly or too lowly of myself. — 0 1 2 3 4 5

31. I believe the God of the Bible is one in essence but distinct in person — Father, Son, and Holy Spirit. — 0 1 2 3 4 5

32. I believe pain and suffering can often bring me closer to God. — 0 1 2 3 4 5

33. I believe nothing I do or have done can earn my salvation. — 0 1 2 3 4 5

34. I believe the words of the Bible are words from God. — 0 1 2 3 4 5

35. I believe that I exist to know, love, and serve God. — 0 1 2 3 4 5

Personal Assessment

	Does not apply at all		Applies somewhat		Applies completely	

36. I believe I cannot grow as a Christian unless I am an active member of a local church.

0 1 2 3 4 5

37. I believe we are created in the image of God and therefore have equal value, regardless of race, religion, or gender.

0 1 2 3 4 5

38. I believe I am responsible before God to show compassion to the sick and imprisoned.

0 1 2 3 4 5

39. I believe a Christian should live a sacrificial life, not driven by pursuit of material things.

0 1 2 3 4 5

40. I believe that people who deliberately reject Jesus Christ as Savior will not inherit eternal life.

0 1 2 3 4 5

41. I attend religious services and worship with other believers each week.

0 1 2 3 4 5

42. I regularly confess my sins to God.

0 1 2 3 4 5

43. I regularly study the Bible to find direction for my life.

0 1 2 3 4 5

44. I see every aspect of my life and work as service to God.

0 1 2 3 4 5

45. I give up what I want to meet the needs of others.

0 1 2 3 4 5

46. I participate in a group of Christians who really know me and support me.

0 1 2 3 4 5

47. I regularly use my spiritual gift(s) in ministry to accomplish God's purposes.

0 1 2 3 4 5

48. I spend a good deal of time helping people with physical, emotional, or other kinds of needs.

0 1 2 3 4 5

49. I regularly give money to serve and help others.

0 1 2 3 4 5

50. I try to live so that others will see Christ in my life.

0 1 2 3 4 5

51. I rejoice when good things happen to other people.

0 1 2 3 4 5

Personal Assessment

	Does not apply at all		Applies somewhat		Applies completely

52. Circumstances do not dictate my mood.

0 1 2 3 4 5

53. I am not angry with God, myself, or others.

0 1 2 3 4 5

54. I do not burst out in anger toward others.

0 1 2 3 4 5

55. I am confident that God is working everything out for my good, regardless of the circumstances today.

0 1 2 3 4 5

56. I am known to maintain honesty and integrity when under pressure.

0 1 2 3 4 5

57. I am known as a person who speaks words of kindness to those in need of encouragement.

0 1 2 3 4 5

58. I discipline my thoughts based on my faith in Jesus Christ.

0 1 2 3 4 5

59. I am known as a person who is sensitive to the needs of others.

0 1 2 3 4 5

60. I am not known as a person who brags.

0 1 2 3 4 5

61. I believe Jesus is God in the flesh — who died and rose bodily from the dead.

0 1 2 3 4 5

62. I believe God is actively involved in my life.

0 1 2 3 4 5

63. I believe salvation comes only through Jesus Christ.

0 1 2 3 4 5

64. I believe the Bible has decisive authority over what I say and do.

0 1 2 3 4 5

65. I believe God loves me, even when I do not obey him.

0 1 2 3 4 5

66. I believe the community of true believers is Christ's body on earth.

0 1 2 3 4 5

67. I believe all people are loved by God; therefore, I too should love them.

0 1 2 3 4 5

68. I believe I should stand up for those who cannot stand up for themselves.

0 1 2 3 4 5

69. I believe Christians should give at least 10 percent of their income to God's work.

0 1 2 3 4 5

Personal Assessment

	Does not apply at all		Applies somewhat		Applies completely
70. I believe that every person is subject to the judgment of God.	0	1	2	3	4 5
71. I give God credit for all that I am and all that I possess.	0	1	2	3	4 5
72. Prayer is a central part of my daily life.	0	1	2	3	4 5
73. I seek to be obedient to God by applying the truth of the Bible to my life.	0	1	2	3	4 5
74. I spend time each day reading God's Word and praying.	0	1	2	3	4 5
75. I give away things I possess when I am so led by God.	0	1	2	3	4 5
76. I allow other Christians to hold me accountable for my actions.	0	1	2	3	4 5
77. I value the spiritual gifts of others to accomplish God's purposes.	0	1	2	3	4 5
78. I give away my time to serve and help others in my community.	0	1	2	3	4 5
79. My first priority in spending is to support God's work.	0	1	2	3	4 5
80. I know how to share my faith with non-Christians.	0	1	2	3	4 5
81. I demonstrate love equally toward people of all races.	0	1	2	3	4 5
82. I am excited about the sense of purpose I have for my life.	0	1	2	3	4 5
83. I forgive people who deeply hurt me.	0	1	2	3	4 5
84. I do not have sexual relationships that are contrary to biblical teaching.	0	1	2	3	4 5
85. My hope in God increases through my daily pursuit to live like Christ.	0	1	2	3	4 5
86. I always put matters into God's hands when I am under pressure.	0	1	2	3	4 5
87. I give to others expecting nothing in return.	0	1	2	3	4 5
88. I follow God even when it involves suffering.	0	1	2	3	4 5

Personal Assessment

	Does not apply at all		Applies somewhat		Applies completely

89. I am known for not raising my voice.
0 1 2 3 4 5

90. I am willing to make any of my faults known to Christians who care for me.
0 1 2 3 4 5

91. I believe the Holy Spirit is God and dwells in Christians to empower them to live the Christian life.
0 1 2 3 4 5

92. I believe God enables me to do things I could not or would not otherwise do.
0 1 2 3 4 5

93. I believe people are saved because of what Jesus Christ did, not because of what they do.
0 1 2 3 4 5

94. I believe the Bible is relevant to address the needs of contemporary culture.
0 1 2 3 4 5

95. I believe I am forgiven and accepted by God.
0 1 2 3 4 5

96. I believe the purpose of the church is to share the gospel and nurture Christians to maturity in Christ.
0 1 2 3 4 5

97. I believe God desires all people to have a relationship with Jesus Christ.
0 1 2 3 4 5

98. I believe Christians should not purchase everything they can afford, so that their discretionary money might be available to help those in need.
0 1 2 3 4 5

99. I believe God will bless Christians now and in the life to come for their good works.
0 1 2 3 4 5

100. I believe all people who place their trust in Jesus Christ will spend eternity in heaven.
0 1 2 3 4 5

101. I am not ashamed for others to know that I worship God.
0 1 2 3 4 5

102. I seek to grow closer to God by listening to him in prayer.
0 1 2 3 4 5

103. I have a good understanding of the contents of the Bible.
0 1 2 3 4 5

Personal Assessment

	Does not apply at all		Applies somewhat		Applies completely

104. I value a simple lifestyle over one cluttered with activities and material possessions.

0 1 2 3 4 5

105. I serve God through my daily work.

0 1 2 3 4 5

106. I daily pray for and support other Christians.

0 1 2 3 4 5

107. Others recognize and affirm my spiritual gift(s) and support my use of them.

0 1 2 3 4 5

108. I regularly volunteer at my church.

0 1 2 3 4 5

109. My spending habits do not keep me from giving what I feel I should give to God.

0 1 2 3 4 5

110. I pray for non-Christians to accept Jesus Christ as their Lord and Savior.

0 1 2 3 4 5

111. I frequently give up what I want for the sake of others.

0 1 2 3 4 5

112. I can be content with the money and possessions I now have.

0 1 2 3 4 5

113. I have an inner peace from God.

0 1 2 3 4 5

114. I control my tongue.

0 1 2 3 4 5

115. My hope for the future is not found in my health or wealth because both are so uncertain, but in God.

0 1 2 3 4 5

116. I keep my composure even when people or circumstances irritate me.

0 1 2 3 4 5

117. I help those who are in trouble or who cannot help themselves.

0 1 2 3 4 5

118. I follow through on commitments I have made to God.

0 1 2 3 4 5

119. I allow people to make mistakes.

0 1 2 3 4 5

120. I am not upset when my achievements are not recognized.

0 1 2 3 4 5

Congratulations!

You've taken a very important first step in identifying where you are right now in your Christian life! While the material is fresh in your mind and heart, try to capture some of the details as they relate to your experience in taking the assessment. This is simply to help you understand your thoughts, feelings, and what God may be saying to you through this personal reflection. Take just a moment and write down any memories that came to you and any areas or statements that seemed particularly sensitive or painful. Lastly, capture any thoughts or emotions you feel called to take action on now. When you finish, go to the next section, where you will begin to measure your answers.

MEASURING
THE RESULTS

Measuring the Results

Instructions

Transfer your responses from pages 23–29 to the Scoring Table on next page. For example, if your response to question one was a "3," record that number in the space next to "1."

When you have completed transferring your responses to the Scoring Table, add the rows of answers horizontally across the page (as indicated by the arrows in the sample below), writing your answer in the space to the right of the Key Idea associated with that row. Then, beginning at the zero (0) on the bar graph next to your total for each row, darken the line moving to the right until you reach your score for that Key Idea. Repeat this process for each of the thirty rows of answers.

Sample Scoring Table

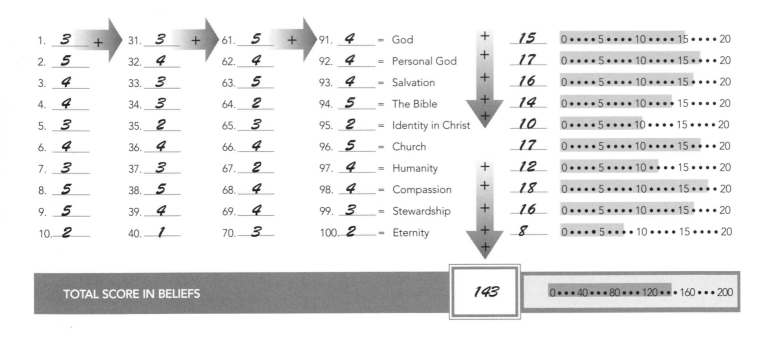

Once you've completed the horizontal scoring, begin adding the individual Key Idea totals vertically, placing the sum in the box beneath the last Key Idea (143 in the sample above). Do this for your scores in Beliefs, Practices, and Virtues.

Scoring Table

1. _____	31. _____	61. _____	91. _____	= God	_____	0 • • • • 5 • • • • 10 • • • • 15 • • • • 20
2. _____	32. _____	62. _____	92. _____	= Personal God	_____	0 • • • • 5 • • • • 10 • • • • 15 • • • • 20
3. _____	33. _____	63. _____	93. _____	= Salvation	_____	0 • • • • 5 • • • • 10 • • • • 15 • • • • 20
4. _____	34. _____	64. _____	94. _____	– The Bible	_____	0 • • • • 5 • • • • 10 • • • • 15 • • • • 20
5. _____	35. _____	65. _____	95. _____	= Identity in Christ	_____	0 • • • • 5 • • • • 10 • • • • 15 • • • • 20
6. _____	36. _____	66. _____	96. _____	= Church	_____	0 • • • • 5 • • • • 10 • • • • 15 • • • • 20
7. _____	37. _____	67. _____	97. _____	= Humanity	_____	0 • • • • 5 • • • • 10 • • • • 15 • • • • 20
8. _____	38. _____	68. _____	98. _____	= Compassion	_____	0 • • • • 5 • • • • 10 • • • • 15 • • • • 20
9. _____	39. _____	69. _____	99. _____	= Stewardship	_____	0 • • • • 5 • • • • 10 • • • • 15 • • • • 20
10. _____	40. _____	70. _____	100. _____	= Eternity	_____	0 • • • • 5 • • • • 10 • • • • 15 • • • • 20

TOTAL SCORE IN BELIEFS   [ ]   0 • • • 40 • • • 80 • • • 120 • • • 160 • • • 200

11. _____	41. _____	71. _____	101. _____	= Worship	_____	0 • • • • 5 • • • • 10 • • • • 15 • • • • 20
12. _____	42. _____	72. _____	102. _____	– Prayer	_____	0 • • • • 5 • • • • 10 • • • • 15 • • • • 20
13. _____	43. _____	73. _____	103. _____	= Bible Study	_____	0 • • • • 5 • • • • 10 • • • • 15 • • • • 20
14. _____	44. _____	74. _____	104. _____	= Single-Mindedness	_____	0 • • • • 5 • • • • 10 • • • • 15 • • • • 20
15. _____	45. _____	75. _____	105. _____	= Total Surrender	_____	0 • • • • 5 • • • • 10 • • • • 15 • • • • 20
16. _____	46. _____	76. _____	106. _____	= Biblical Community	_____	0 • • • • 5 • • • • 10 • • • • 15 • • • • 20
17. _____	47. _____	77. _____	107. _____	= Spiritual Gifts	_____	0 • • • • 5 • • • • 10 • • • • 15 • • • • 20
18. _____	48. _____	78. _____	108. _____	= Offering My Time	_____	0 • • • • 5 • • • • 10 • • • • 15 • • • • 20
19. _____	49. _____	79. _____	109. _____	= Giving My Resources	_____	0 • • • • 5 • • • • 10 • • • • 15 • • • • 20
20. _____	50. _____	80. _____	110. _____	= Sharing My Faith	_____	0 • • • • 5 • • • • 10 • • • • 15 • • • • 20

TOTAL SCORE IN PRACTICES   [ ]   0 • • • 40 • • • 80 • • • 120 • • • 160 • • • 200

21. _____	51. _____	81. _____	111. _____	= Love	_____	0 • • • • 5 • • • • 10 • • • • 15 • • • • 20
22. _____	52. _____	82. _____	112. _____	= Joy	_____	0 • • • • 5 • • • • 10 • • • • 15 • • • • 20
23. _____	53. _____	83. _____	113. _____	= Peace	_____	0 • • • • 5 • • • • 10 • • • • 15 • • • • 20
24. _____	54. _____	84. _____	114. _____	= Self-Control	_____	0 • • • • 5 • • • • 10 • • • • 15 • • • • 20
25. _____	55. _____	85. _____	115. _____	= Hope	_____	0 • • • • 5 • • • • 10 • • • • 15 • • • • 20
26. _____	56. _____	86. _____	116. _____	= Patience	_____	0 • • • • 5 • • • • 10 • • • • 15 • • • • 20
27. _____	57. _____	87. _____	117. _____	= Kindness/Goodness	_____	0 • • • • 5 • • • • 10 • • • • 15 • • • • 20
28. _____	58. _____	88. _____	118. _____	= Faithfulness	_____	0 • • • • 5 • • • • 10 • • • • 15 • • • • 20
29. _____	59. _____	89. _____	119. _____	= Gentleness	_____	0 • • • • 5 • • • • 10 • • • • 15 • • • • 20
30. _____	60. _____	90. _____	120. _____	= Humility	_____	0 • • • • 5 • • • • 10 • • • • 15 • • • • 20

TOTAL SCORE IN VIRTUES   [ ]   0 • • • 40 • • • 80 • • • 120 • • • 160 • • • 200

"ONE ANOTHER" ASSESSMENTS

What Is a "One Another" Assessment?

Instructions

The New Testament includes a series of instructions to Christians that include the words "one another" (e.g., encourage one another, confess to one another, be devoted to one another, love one another, instruct one another). It takes a community to properly and effectively grow to think, act, and be like Jesus.

The "One Another" assessments are a vital part of a balanced personal assessment. The "One Another" assessments are based exclusively on the Virtue key ideas. The Beliefs and Practices categories would be difficult for another person to accurately assess.

It is recommended that you carefully choose the people to whom you provide your assessments. Choose people who know you well and whose opinion you trust and respect.

The goal is to discover the truth about your Christian life. You can't grow if you don't know. You may select a variety of people to complete your assessments (i.e., a family member, a person from your church or small group, a coworker, a neighbor, or a friend). Take the feedback provided as opportunities to personally grow and to become even closer to the people you've chosen to comment on your Christian walk.

Remove the perforated "One Another" assessments from the book and ask the people you've selected to complete and return the assessments by a specific date. Encourage them to be as completely honest as possible.

Do not look at these assessments until after you've completed your self-assessment and tabulated the results on page 33.

When you receive the "One Another" assessments, transpose the answers from the individual assessments to the "Scoring the Feedback" section on page 43. Score the results in the same way as you did with your personal assessment, first adding across horizontally to determine a Key Idea score and then adding the totals vertically to determine a total score. Also, plot the score on the bar graphs for each of the categories.

Keep in mind that the people you choose will most likely score you higher than you do yourself. With the "One Another" feedback you're not so much looking for a total numeric score as for variations in the score. For example, if someone gave you all 5s on thirty-nine of the forty questions and only one 4, this is very significant and gives you feedback regarding an area on which you need to work.

After you finish tabulating the results of your "One Another" assessments, you are ready to develop a personal plan for spiritual growth (pages 46 – 49).

"One Another" Assessment

| Completed by _____ | for _____ | Date _____ |

Instructions

Based on your own impressions and observations of this person's life, respond to each of the following statements. Your responses will provide valuable feedback regarding the qualities or characteristics you have or have not seen portrayed in the life of the person who asked for your assessment. On a scale from 0 (Does not apply at all) to 5 (Applies completely), how accurate are the following statements when applied to the person who asked for your assessment?

		Does not apply at all	Applies somewhat			Applies completely
1.	God's grace enables him/her to forgive people who have hurt him/her.	0 1 2 3 4 5
2.	He/she has an inner contentment even when things go wrong.	0 1 2 3 4 5
3.	He/she knows God has forgiven him/her because of what Jesus has done.	0 1 2 3 4 5
4.	He/she is not addicted to any substances — whether food, caffeine, tobacco, alcohol, or chemical.	0 1 2 3 4 5
5.	He/she thinks a great deal about heaven and what God is preparing for him/her as a Christian.	0 1 2 3 4 5
6.	He/she does not get angry with God when he/she has to endure suffering.	0 1 2 3 4 5
7.	He/she would never keep money that didn't belong to him/her.	0 1 2 3 4 5
8.	He/she takes unpopular stands when his/her faith dictates.	0 1 2 3 4 5
9.	He/she considers his/her own shortcomings when faced with the failures of others.	0 1 2 3 4 5
10.	As a child of God, he/she does not think too highly or too lowly of himself/herself.	0 1 2 3 4 5
11.	He/she rejoices when good things happen to other people.	0 1 2 3 4 5
12.	Circumstances do not dictate his/her mood.	0 1 2 3 4 5
13.	He/she is not angry with God, himself/herself, or others.	0 1 2 3 4 5
14.	He/she does not burst out in anger toward others.	0 1 2 3 4 5
15.	He/she is confident that God is working everything out for his/her good, regardless of the circumstances today.	0 1 2 3 4 5
16.	He/she is known to maintain honesty and integrity when under pressure.	0 1 2 3 4 5
17.	He/she is known as a person who speaks words of kindness to those in need of encouragement.	0 1 2 3 4 5

"One Another" Assessment

	Does not apply at all		Applies somewhat		Applies completely
18. He/she disciplines his/her thoughts based on his/her faith in Jesus Christ.	0	1	2	3	4	5
19. He/she is known as a person who is sensitive to the needs of others.	0	1	2	3	4	5
20. He/she is not known as a person who brags.	0	1	2	3	4	5
21. He/she demonstrates love equally toward people of all races.	0	1	2	3	4	5
22. He/she is excited about the sense of purpose he/she has for his/her life.	0	1	2	3	4	5
23. He/she forgives people who deeply hurt him/her.	0	1	2	3	4	5
24. He/she does not have sexual relationships that are contrary to biblical teaching.	0	1	2	3	4	5
25. His/her hope in God increases through his/her daily pursuit to live like Christ.	0	1	2	3	4	5
26. He/she always puts matters into God's hands when he/she is under pressure.	0	1	2	3	4	5
27. He/she gives to others expecting nothing in return.	0	1	2	3	4	5
28. He/she follows God even when it involves suffering.	0	1	2	3	4	5
29. He/she is known for not raising his/her voice.	0	1	2	3	4	5
30. He/she is willing to make any of his/her faults known to Christians who care for him/her.	0	1	2	3	4	5
31. He/she frequently gives up what he/she wants for the sake of others.	0	1	2	3	4	5
32. He/she can be content with the money and possessions he/she now has.	0	1	2	3	4	5
33. He/she has an inner peace from God.	0	1	2	3	4	5
34. He/she controls his/her tongue.	0	1	2	3	4	5
35. His/her hope for the future is not found in his/her health or wealth because both are so uncertain, but in God.	0	1	2	3	4	5
36. He/she keeps his/her composure even when people or circumstances irritate him/her.	0	1	2	3	4	5
37. He/she helps those who are in trouble or who cannot help themselves.	0	1	2	3	4	5
38. He/she follows through on commitments he/she has made to God.	0	1	2	3	4	5
39. He/she allows people to make mistakes.	0	1	2	3	4	5
40. He/she is not upset when his/her achievements are not recognized.	0	1	2	3	4	5

"One Another" Assessment

Completed by _____ for _____ Date _____

Instructions

Based on your own impressions and observations of this person's life, respond to each of the following statements. Your responses will provide valuable feedback regarding the qualities or characteristics you have or have not seen portrayed in the life of the person who asked for your assessment. On a scale from 0 (Does not apply at all) to 5 (Applies completely), how accurate are the following statements when applied to the person who asked for your assessment?

		Does not apply at all		Applies somewhat		Applies completely	
1.	God's grace enables him/her to forgive people who have hurt him/her.	0	1	2	3	4	5
2.	He/she has an inner contentment even when things go wrong.	0	1	2	3	4	5
3.	He/she knows God has forgiven him/her because of what Jesus has done.	0	1	2	3	4	5
4.	He/she is not addicted to any substances – whether food, caffeine, tobacco, alcohol, or chemical.	0	1	2	3	4	5
5.	He/she thinks a great deal about heaven and what God is preparing for him/her as a Christian.	0	1	2	3	4	5
6.	He/she does not get angry with God when he/she has to endure suffering.	0	1	2	3	4	5
7.	He/she would never keep money that didn't belong to him/her.	0	1	2	3	4	5
8.	He/she takes unpopular stands when his/her faith dictates.	0	1	2	3	4	5
9.	He/she considers his/her own shortcomings when faced with the failures of others.	0	1	2	3	4	5
10.	As a child of God, he/she does not think too highly or too lowly of himself/herself.	0	1	2	3	4	5
11	He/she rejoices when good things happen to other people.	0	1	2	3	4	5
12.	Circumstances do not dictate his/her mood.	0	1	2	3	4	5
13.	He/she is not angry with God, himself/herself, or others.	0	1	2	3	4	5
14.	He/she does not burst out in anger toward others.	0	1	2	3	4	5
15.	He/she is confident that God is working everything out for his/her good, regardless of the circumstances today.	0	1	2	3	4	5
16.	He/she is known to maintain honesty and integrity when under pressure.	0	1	2	3	4	5
17.	He/she is known as a person who speaks words of kindness to those in need of encouragement.	0	1	2	3	4	5

"One Another" Assessment

	Does not apply at all		Applies somewhat		Applies completely
	0 1	2	3	4	5

18. He/she disciplines his/her thoughts based on his/her faith in Jesus Christ. 0 1 2 3 4 5

19. He/she is known as a person who is sensitive to the needs of others. 0 1 2 3 4 5

20. He/she is not known as a person who brags. 0 1 2 3 4 5

21. He/she demonstrates love equally toward people of all races. 0 1 2 3 4 5

22. He/she is excited about the sense of purpose he/she has for his/her life. 0 1 2 3 4 5

23. He/she forgives people who deeply hurt him/her. 0 1 2 3 4 5

24. He/she does not have sexual relationships that are contrary to biblical teaching. 0 1 2 3 4 5

25. His/her hope in God increases through his/her daily pursuit to live like Christ. 0 1 2 3 4 5

26. He/she always puts matters into God's hands when he/she is under pressure. 0 1 2 3 4 5

27. He/she gives to others expecting nothing in return. 0 1 2 3 4 5

28. He/she follows God even when it involves suffering. 0 1 2 3 4 5

29. He/she is known for not raising his/her voice. 0 1 2 3 4 5

30. He/she is willing to make any of his/her faults known to Christians who care for him/her. 0 1 2 3 4 5

31. He/she frequently gives up what he/she wants for the sake of others. 0 1 2 3 4 5

32. He/she can be content with the money and possessions he/she now has. 0 1 2 3 4 5

33. He/she has an inner peace from God. 0 1 2 3 4 5

34. He/she controls his/her tongue. 0 1 2 3 4 5

35. His/her hope for the future is not found in his/her health or wealth because both are so uncertain, but in God. 0 1 2 3 4 5

36. He/she keeps his/her composure even when people or circumstances irritate him/her. 0 1 2 3 4 5

37. He/she helps those who are in trouble or who cannot help themselves. 0 1 2 3 4 5

38. He/she follows through on commitments he/she has made to God. 0 1 2 3 4 5

39. He/she allows people to make mistakes. 0 1 2 3 4 5

40. He/she is not upset when his/her achievements are not recognized. 0 1 2 3 4 5

"One Another" Assessment

| Completed by _____ | for _____ | Date _____ |

Instructions

Based on your own impressions and observations of this person's life, respond to each of the following statements. Your responses will provide valuable feedback regarding the qualities or characteristics you have or have not seen portrayed in the life of the person who asked for your assessment. On a scale from 0 (Does not apply at all) to 5 (Applies completely), how accurate are the following statements when applied to the person who asked for your assessment?

		Does not apply at all		Applies somewhat		Applies completely	
1.	God's grace enables him/her to forgive people who have hurt him/her.	0	1	2	3	4	5
2.	He/she has an inner contentment even when things go wrong.	0	1	2	3	4	5
3.	He/she knows God has forgiven him/her because of what Jesus has done.	0	1	2	3	4	5
4.	He/she is not addicted to any substances — whether food, caffeine, tobacco, alcohol, or chemical.	0	1	2	3	4	5
5.	He/she thinks a great deal about heaven and what God is preparing for him/her as a Christian.	0	1	2	3	4	5
6.	He/she does not get angry with God when he/she has to endure suffering.	0	1	2	3	4	5
7.	He/she would never keep money that didn't belong to him/her.	0	1	2	3	4	5
8.	He/she takes unpopular stands when his/her faith dictates.	0	1	2	3	4	5
9.	He/she considers his/her own shortcomings when faced with the failures of others.	0	1	2	3	4	5
10.	As a child of God, he/she does not think too highly or too lowly of himself/herself.	0	1	2	3	4	5
11.	He/she rejoices when good things happen to other people.	0	1	2	3	4	5
12.	Circumstances do not dictate his/her mood.	0	1	2	3	4	5
13.	He/she is not angry with God, himself/herself, or others.	0	1	2	3	4	5
14.	He/she does not burst out in anger toward others.	0	1	2	3	4	5
15.	He/she is confident that God is working everything out for his/her good, regardless of the circumstances today.	0	1	2	3	4	5
16.	He/she is known to maintain honesty and integrity when under pressure.	0	1	2	3	4	5
17.	He/she is known as a person who speaks words of kindness to those in need of encouragement.	0	1	2	3	4	5

"One Another" Assessment

		Does not apply at all		Applies somewhat			Applies completely
18.	He/she disciplines his/her thoughts based on his/her faith in Jesus Christ.	0	1	2	3	4	5
19.	He/she is known as a person who is sensitive to the needs of others.	0	1	2	3	4	5
20.	He/she is not known as a person who brags.	0	1	2	3	4	5
21.	He/she demonstrates love equally toward people of all races.	0	1	2	3	4	5
22.	He/she is excited about the sense of purpose he/she has for his/her life.	0	1	2	3	4	5
23.	He/she forgives people who deeply hurt him/her.	0	1	2	3	4	5
24.	He/she does not have sexual relationships that are contrary to biblical teaching.	0	1	2	3	4	5
25.	His/her hope in God increases through his/her daily pursuit to live like Christ.	0	1	2	3	4	5
26.	He/she always puts matters into God's hands when he/she is under pressure.	0	1	2	3	4	5
27.	He/she gives to others expecting nothing in return.	0	1	2	3	4	5
28.	He/she follows God even when it involves suffering.	0	1	2	3	4	5
29.	He/she is known for not raising his/her voice.	0	1	2	3	4	5
30.	He/she is willing to make any of his/her faults known to Christians who care for him/her.	0	1	2	3	4	5
31.	He/she frequently gives up what he/she wants for the sake of others.	0	1	2	3	4	5
32.	He/she can be content with the money and possessions he/she now has.	0	1	2	3	4	5
33.	He/she has an inner peace from God.	0	1	2	3	4	5
34.	He/she controls his/her tongue.	0	1	2	3	4	5
35.	His/her hope for the future is not found in his/her health or wealth because both are so uncertain, but in God.	0	1	2	3	4	5
36.	He/she keeps his/her composure even when people or circumstances irritate him/her.	0	1	2	3	4	5
37.	He/she helps those who are in trouble or who cannot help themselves.	0	1	2	3	4	5
38.	He/she follows through on commitments he/she has made to God.	0	1	2	3	4	5
39.	He/she allows people to make mistakes.	0	1	2	3	4	5
40.	He/she is not upset when his/her achievements are not recognized.	0	1	2	3	4	5

Scoring the Feedback

ONE ANOTHER

1. ___	11. ___	21. ___	31. ___	= Love	___	0 • • • • 5 • • • 10 • • • • 15 • • • • 20
2. ___	12. ___	22. ___	32. ___	= Joy		0 • • • • 5 • • • 10 • • • • 15 • • • • 20
3. ___	13. ___	23. ___	33. ___	= Peace		0 • • • • 5 • • • 10 • • • • 15 • • • • 20
4. ___	14. ___	24. ___	34. ___	= Patience		0 • • • • 5 • • • 10 • • • • 15 • • • • 20
5. ___	15. ___	25. ___	35. ___	= Kindness/Goodness	___	0 • • • • 5 • • • 10 • • • • 15 • • • • 20
6. ___	16. ___	26. ___	36. ___	= Faithfulness		0 • • • • 5 • • • 10 • • • • 15 • • • • 20
7. ___	17. ___	27. ___	37. ___	= Gentleness		0 • • • • 5 • • • 10 • • • • 15 • • • • 20
8. ___	18. ___	28. ___	38. ___	= Self-Control		0 • • • • 5 • • • 10 • • • • 15 • • • • 20
9. ___	19. ___	29. ___	39. ___	= Hope		0 • • • • 5 • • • 10 • • • • 15 • • • • 20
10. ___	20. ___	30. ___	40. ___	= Humility		0 • • • • 5 • • • 10 • • • • 15 • • • • 20

TOTAL SCORE IN VIRTUES   [ ]   0 • • • 40 • • • 80 • • • 120 • • • 160 • • • 200

ONE ANOTHER

1. ___	11. ___	21. ___	31. ___	= Love	___	0 • • • • 5 • • • 10 • • • • 15 • • • • 20
2. ___	12. ___	22. ___	32. ___	= Joy		0 • • • • 5 • • • 10 • • • • 15 • • • • 20
3. ___	13. ___	23. ___	33. ___	= Peace		0 • • • • 5 • • • 10 • • • • 15 • • • • 20
4. ___	14. ___	24. ___	34. ___	= Patience		0 • • • • 5 • • • 10 • • • • 15 • • • • 20
5. ___	15. ___	25. ___	35. ___	= Kindness/Goodness	___	0 • • • • 5 • • • 10 • • • • 15 • • • • 20
6. ___	16. ___	26. ___	36. ___	= Faithfulness		0 • • • • 5 • • • 10 • • • • 15 • • • • 20
7. ___	17. ___	27. ___	37. ___	= Gentleness		0 • • • • 5 • • • 10 • • • • 15 • • • • 20
8. ___	18. ___	28. ___	38. ___	= Self-Control		0 • • • • 5 • • • 10 • • • • 15 • • • • 20
9. ___	19. ___	29. ___	39. ___	= Hope		0 • • • • 5 • • • 10 • • • • 15 • • • • 20
10. ___	20. ___	30. ___	40. ___	= Humility		0 • • • • 5 • • • 10 • • • • 15 • • • • 20

TOTAL SCORE IN VIRTUES   [ ]   0 • • • 40 • • • 80 • • • 120 • • • 160 • • • 200

ONE ANOTHER

1. ___	11. ___	21. ___	31. ___	= Love		0 • • • • 5 • • • 10 • • • • 15 • • • • 20
2. ___	12. ___	22. ___	32. ___	= Joy		0 • • • • 5 • • • 10 • • • • 15 • • • • 20
3. ___	13. ___	23. ___	33. ___	= Peace		0 • • • • 5 • • • 10 • • • • 15 • • • • 20
4. ___	14. ___	24. ___	34. ___	= Self-Control		0 • • • • 5 • • • 10 • • • • 15 • • • • 20
5. ___	15. ___	25. ___	35. ___	= Hope		0 • • • • 5 • • • 10 • • • • 15 • • • • 20
6. ___	16. ___	26. ___	36. ___	= Patience		0 • • • • 5 • • • 10 • • • • 15 • • • • 20
7. ___	17. ___	27. ___	37. ___	= Kindness/Goodness		0 • • • • 5 • • • 10 • • • • 15 • • • • 20
8. ___	18. ___	28. ___	38. ___	= Faithfulness		0 • • • • 5 • • • 10 • • • • 15 • • • • 20
9. ___	19. ___	29. ___	39. ___	= Gentleness		0 • • • • 5 • • • 10 • • • • 15 • • • • 20
10. ___	20. ___	30. ___	40. ___	= Humility		0 • • • • 5 • • • 10 • • • • 15 • • • • 20

TOTAL SCORE IN VIRTUES   [ ]   0 • • • 40 • • • 80 • • • 120 • • • 160 • • • 200

PERSONAL PLAN FOR SPIRITUAL GROWTH

Personal Plan for Spiritual Growth

Instructions

Now that you've completed your personal assessment and solicited the feedback of three other people, you are ready to develop a targeted plan for spiritual growth.

Remember, God desires to work a healthy balance into our lives; so we want to discover the areas in our Christian experience where we are deficient. So many Christians continue to build only on their strengths and never address areas of weakness. The objective is to discover where in your life God wants to initiate change, and then develop a goal for personal growth, along with a specific, measurable plan to realize this goal.

Celebrating Your Strengths

1. Looking at your personal assessment score (page 33), what is your strongest competency in each area? After each one, summarize your thoughts on why this is an area of strength for you.

   Beliefs: _____

   Practices: _____

   Virtues: _____

2. Looking at the scores for your "One Another" assessments (page 43), add together the three scores for each virtue. In what three areas were you scored the highest? After each one, summarize your thoughts on why this is an area of strength for you.

   Virtue: _____

   Virtue: _____

   Virtue: _____

3. Compare your personal assessment of your strengths with the "One Anothers." Are they the same? Are they different? Record your thoughts below. _____

   _____

   _____

   _____

Targeting Your Growth Area

1. Looking at your personal assessment score (page 33), what are your lowest scores in each area? After each one, summarize your thoughts on why this is an area of weakness for you. Look at your scores for each individual statement. Is there a belief, practice, or virtue on which you scored particularly low on one statement as compared to the other three? If so, look back at that assessment statement and write it in the space provided below. This will aid you in targeting a more specific area for growth.

   Beliefs: _____

Personal Plan for Spiritual Growth

Practices: _____

_____

Virtues: _____

_____

2. Do you see any relationship or connection between these three areas? _____

_____

_____

3. Looking at the scores for your "One Another" assessments (page 43), in what three areas did your assessors score you the lowest? A good idea is to probe with them in person why they gave you low ratings in this area. Make sure you give them the freedom to share frankly with you. After each of the three areas, summarize their thoughts on why this is an area of weakness for you. If there is one statement for which they scored you particularly low as compared to the other three statements in a given area, write that statement in the space provided below. This will aid you in targeting a more specific area for growth.

Virtue: _____

_____

Virtue: _____

_____

Virtue: _____

_____

4. Compare the lowest area on your personal assessment with the "One Anothers." Are they the same? Are they different? Record your thoughts below. _____

_____

_____

_____

5. In the space below, identify just one Key Idea you desire to concentrate on over the next year. If it is one specific statement from the assessment, write that down as well. It can be a belief, a practice, or a virtue. Before you make your final selection, spend time in meditation and prayer. Explain why you chose this particular Key Idea. _____

_____

_____

_____

Personal Plan for Spiritual Growth

My Personal Plan for Spiritual Growth

Today's Date: _____

Over the next twelve months, I, _____ ,
                                        (insert your name)

with the help of my God and community, intend to grow in the area of:

_____
                (category, Key Idea, specific statement)

by (record specific action steps you have identified after working through the material on page 54):

1. _____

2. _____

3. _____

4. _____

5. _____

The three people I am asking to encourage me, pray for me, and hold me accountable to accomplish
this goal are:

Name: _____ Signature of Person: _____

Name: _____ Signature of Person: _____

Name: _____ Signature of Person: _____

How did I do? (One year from now sit down with the three people above and evaluate your progress.
Record your combined thoughts below.) _____

_____

_____

_____

_____

_____

_____

_____

_____

Personal Plan for Spiritual Growth

My Personal Plan for Growth
(Read This Page First!)

1. Refer to "My Personal Plan for Spiritual Growth" on page 48. Take a moment now to reflect on the area you've targeted. First, write out the category (Beliefs, Practices, Virtues). Second, identify the Key Idea (for example, God, Prayer, Peace). Finally, if applicable, write out the specific statement you are targeting (for example, "I allow people to make mistakes" [Q. #119]). If there is not one specific question, simply write down the statement for that Key Idea for that area found on pages 14–19 (for example, "I am thoughtful, considerate, and calm in my dealings with others" [Key Idea for Gentleness]).

2. Now carefully read pages 53–54, which will help you understand the relationship between the Beliefs, Practices, and Virtues. For example, while you may have identified a virtue as your targeted area, you may choose a resource in a Beliefs area or Practices area because growth in that area can be essential to maximizing your growth in the virtue selected.

3. Go to the website www.RandyFrazee.com and look at the recommended resources and ideas for the specific area you selected as well as the resources and ideas from the related categories from your discovery above. Select at least one and no more than five specific action steps you intend to take over the next twelve months to grow in your targeted area.

4. Seek out a spiritual mentor to give you guidance on specific things you can do to help you grow in this area. Your mentor might be a parent, a friend you look up to, your small group leader, a Sunday school teacher, or your pastor or priest. Share with them your desire to grow in this area and ask them what they would recommend to help you along the way. It may be a book to read, a class to attend, an activity to engage in, a song to hear, or another person to talk to.

5. Identify three people to help you through prayer, encouragement, and gentle accountability. Ask them to sign their name on the appropriate line. Make a copy of your personal plan for each of them to keep.

6. Share your discoveries and your personal plan for spiritual growth with the members of your small group.

7. Keep your personal plan in a place where you can review it regularly (in your Bible, in your planner, posted on a bulletin board). Lay this plan before you as you pray, asking God for insight, discipline, and strength.

8. In one year evaluate your progress, recording your thoughts in the space provided on page 48. Don't forget to include feedback from the three people you asked to help you accomplish this goal.

RESOURCES FOR TARGETED GROWTH

Resources for Targeted Growth

This section of the Christian Life Profile assessment guides you in selecting specific action steps that will help you grow in your targeted area. In a moment you will be looking at some recommended ideas, suggestions, and resources for the Key Idea you desire to develop. Your objective here is to select from one to five action steps to cultivate growth. You will record them in your personal plan for spiritual growth on page 48.

Before you do so, you'll want to probe the connection between the Beliefs, Practices, and Virtues. Most people will score themselves the highest in Beliefs and the lowest in Practices and Virtues. How about you? Look back at your scores to see if this was true for you.

Beliefs, Practices, and Virtues development all work together to grow your Christian Profile. Consider the diagram below:

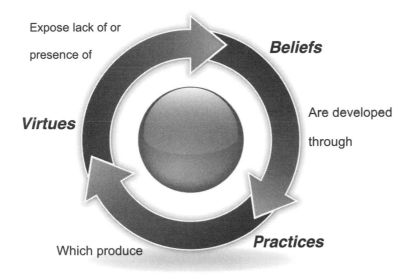

We are what we believe in our heart. We score ourselves high in Beliefs because we understand the concept of a belief or believe in our head that it is the right answer. But until a belief takes the twelve-inch journey from our head to our heart, that belief has little impact on our Christian development. The Practices not only help us live out the Christian life but help move a belief from our head to our heart. Once we truly "buy in" to the idea, it begins the process of changing who we are from the inside out (i.e., Virtues). Virtues are called "fruit" in the Bible (John 15; Galatians 5:22 – 23). Fruit is external and experienced (tasted) by others around us. Therefore, fruit is the easiest of the three categories to measure. When a particular virtue in our life is either present or lacking, as noted by a loving community around us, it exposes the presence of or lack of a Christian belief system in our heart.

For example, if we struggle in the area of humility, we may want to look at our Identity in Christ score. When our identity is based on our performance and not on our position in Christ, we feel a need to brag and tout our accomplishments or to dominate a conversation. One of the greatest ways to enhance Christlike humility in our lives is to improve our knowledge and belief in our identity in Christ. There are a number of possible connections. Our struggle with worship may have to do with an inadequate view of God. Our struggle with gentleness might involve not seeing other people as God sees them (humanity).

Resources for Targeted Growth

Take some time to probe the gap between your Beliefs, Practices, and Virtues. If you scored high in the Beliefs but low in the Practices or Virtues, look at your scores in the related areas. It is likely that some of your action steps for the next twelve months will come from other areas. For example, if your selected area for targeted growth is worship, you may seek to grow in your belief in the God). The list below is only a partial listing of connections. Feel free to probe other connections. (By the way, it may really help to dialogue out loud with others about this.)

Beliefs	→	Practices	→	Virtues
God		Worship		Humility, Peace, Hope, Love
Personal God		Prayer		Joy, Peace, Love
Salvation		Sharing My Faith		Peace, Love
The Bible		Bible Study		Self-Control, Humility
Identity in Christ		Worship, Prayer		Humility, Joy
Church		Biblical Community, Spiritual Gifts		Faithfulness, Love
Humanity		Sharing My Faith		Love, Gentleness, Patience
Compassion		Offering My Time, Spiritual Gifts		Kindness/Goodness, Patience
Stewardship		Giving My Resources, Total Surrender, Single-Mindedness		Faithfulness, Self-Control
Eternity		Sharing My Faith		Hope, Patience

A GUIDE FOR SMALL GROUP DISCUSSION

A Guide for Small Group Discussion

The Christian Life Profile assessment is optimized when it is shared with a small group of fellow Christians. If you are the leader of a small group, you can use the outline below to assist your group in sharing the results of their assessment with each other.

Preparing

1. James 5:16 tells us, "Confess your sins to each other and pray for each other so that you may be healed. The prayer of a righteous person is powerful and effective." This biblical practice is a missing component in most contemporary Christian communities. The Christian Life Profile assessment seeks to assist in the healthy restoration of this function.

2. Most people in your group should feel comfortable sharing the results of their profile with the whole group. However, you may have some who are too intimidated, are new to the group, or have had a bad experience in the past with vulnerability. As the leader you need to find out which group members will share the results with the entire group. Those who don't feel comfortable should not be pressured. See if they are willing to share the results one-on-one with you, as the leader, or with someone else in the group. Later, when the person is ready, he or she can share with the whole group. Please stress to all group members that everything shared is strictly confidential.

3. Assign a date for people to share their profiles with the group. Essentially, they will be sharing their answers from the "Personal Plan for Spiritual Growth" section (pages 46 – 48). It takes a minimum of thirty minutes and a maximum of sixty minutes to share one profile.

Sharing

1. The person assigned begins by sharing his or her strengths as recorded in the "Personal Plan for Spiritual Growth" section ("Celebrating Your Strengths," page 46).

2. Members of the group should take time to celebrate that person by sharing their positive experiences with him or her. This should be a totally uplifting time for that person. For example, another group member may say, "John, I affirm that you are strong in prayer. I remember a time when …"

3. The person then shares his or her areas of greatest struggle ("Targeting Your Growth Area," pages 46 – 47). It is very important that other group members not dismiss a person's confession. Other members should not say things like, "Oh, I really don't see that in you." Group members should interact and ask questions in a sensitive manner.

4. The person now shares the area in which he or she is trusting God for growth over the next twelve months ("My Personal Plan for Spiritual Growth," page 48). Reinforce the need to have a specific and measurable plan for growing in this area. Also, find out which three people he or she has asked or plans to ask to sign this plan to help him or her reach this goal.

A Guide for Small Group Discussion

Praying

1. When the person is done sharing, gather around that person to pray over him or her.

2. In the prayer, celebrate that person's life, strengths, desire to grow in the selected areas, and the group's commitment to support him or her in this journey.

Probing Deeper

1. If your group desires, you can use the following suggestions to probe the results of the profile more deeply.

2. Probe your assessment for cause-effect relationships. Take an area you scored low in, and look at other Beliefs, Practices, and Virtues that are also low to see what role they may play in influencing your development in this area.

3. Probe the gap between Beliefs, Practices, and Virtues. If you scored high in the Beliefs but low in the Practices or Virtues, then you may want to probe the actual depth of your beliefs. There is a difference between owning a belief in your heart and simply thinking it is the right answer for Christians to embrace. Consider the possible connections below between the Beliefs, Practices, and Virtues.

Beliefs	Practices	Virtues
God	Worship	Humility, Peace, Hope, Love
Personal God	Prayer	Joy, Peace, Love
Salvation	Sharing My Faith	Peace, Love
The Bible	Bible Study	Self-Control, Humility
Identity in Christ	Worship, Prayer	Humility, Joy
Church	Biblical Community, Spiritual Gifts	Faithfulness, Love
Humanity	Sharing My Faith	Love, Gentleness, Patience
Compassion	Offering My Time, Spiritual Gifts	Kindness/Goodness, Patience
Stewardship	Giving My Resources, Total Surrender, Single-Mindedness	Faithfulness, Self-Control
Eternity	Sharing My Faith	Hope, Patience

A Guide for Small Group Discussion

4. Probe the "One Anothers." Take the time to look at your "One Another" assessments globally.

   a. Probe the areas where the "One Anothers" differ.

   For example, if only one person scored you low on the statement "He/she allows people to make mistakes," maybe you only struggle to do this in your relationship with that person. You may want to talk further with him or her about this.

   b. Probe what it may mean if someone gave you all 4s and 5s. It could mean you mentored or discipled that person, and he or she idolizes you. Perhaps it would be wise to have someone else do your assessment as well. It could also mean they don't feel safe telling you the truth. It could simply mean they don't like to be confrontational in any way. Pray about talking to him or her regarding this issue. Keep in mind that most people will rate you higher than you rated yourself. Don't look at the numbers but at the dips in the numbers.

   For example, if they gave you a 5 on most things and then gave you a 4 or 3 in an area, they are likely sending you a big message, even though you may have scored yourself lower.

Following Up

1. Each group member should write down the other members' growth plans on a sheet of paper. You can use the "Prayer Guide for Group Members" on the next page if you like. Be sure to use it respectfully and confidentially. You may encourage everyone to use initials instead of actual names for their list.

2. About once a month, you can ask that person to give an update on how things are going. It's usually a good idea to let them know ahead of time that it will be their turn to share, so they'll be ready to give a good update. Use this as an opportunity to encourage, pray over, or even gently challenge each other.

3. Commit as a group to taking the profile again exactly one year from the time you first took it. Compare the results next year with what happened this year. The findings should be most helpful and encouraging.

Prayer Guide for Group Members

Below is the list of the names (or initials) of the people who took the Christian Life Profile assessment with me. There is space provided for writing down the area they are targeting for growth over the next year. I commit to supporting and praying for them as they take this awesome journey to think, act, and be more like Jesus Christ.

	Name	Area of Targeted Growth	Comments
1.			
2.			
3.			
4.			
5.			
6.			
7.			
8.			
9.			
10.			

The Story behind the Christian Life Profile Assessment

The assessment you hold in your hands has been in development over the last twenty years. It is a labor of love and a passion for Christ of many people.

The Initial Challenge

Bob Buford, founder of Leadership Network and author of *Halftime*, gave the initial challenge to pastors to "measure the mission." If our mission is to produce followers of Christ, said Buford, then we need some indication that it's actually happening in people's lives. I was captivated by this vision and took Buford up on his challenge. As Bob has done with so many projects, he put his money where his mouth is and funded the work. Plain and simple, this would not be in your hands today without Bob's obedience to Christ and his passion to produce "fruit that grows on others' trees."

The Initial Team

Three teams came together to tackle the assignment — Pantego Bible Church, Fort Worth, Texas; Willow Creek Community Church, South Barrington, Illinois; and the South Carolina Southern Baptist Convention. While each of us worked to develop our own model, we freely shared invaluable ideas and insights with each other.

The Source behind the Thirty Key Ideas

The Bible is the sole source behind the selection of the thirty Key Ideas. Dozens of people scrolled through the Bible over and over again to find the core, repeatable characteristics of a follower of Christ. The structure of Beliefs, Practices, and Virtues was birthed out of *The Saints Among Us* by George Gallup Jr. and Timothy Jones. The initial idea of building the thirty Key Ideas around the greatest commandment — love God and love our neighbor — came from Winton Manning, former senior vice president of Educational Testing Service in Princeton, New Jersey.

The Development of the Assessment

The first edition of this assessment was created out of multiple brainstorming meetings I had with George Gallup Jr. in Dallas, Texas, and Princeton, New Jersey. Several people joined us at these gatherings, including Bob Buford, Scott Jones, Alan Klaas, Gerald McDermott, Larry Nelson, and John Williams, to name a few. I have fond memories of the long days in the Gun Room of the Nassau Club with these folks.

Testing and Refining

Several people over the years have graciously offered their input and assistance in making this a first-class assessment. Dallas Willard, J. I. Packer, and Larry Crabb gave insightful feedback on the theology and the recommended communal approach. George Barna gave us feedback on its structure, which took the quality to another level. Alan Klaas tested it in twenty churches to ensure that the questions were effective in helping people identify their spiritual strengths and gaps in their journeys to become followers of Christ. Gerald McDermott gathered an ecumenical group of leaders from the Catholic Church and all the major Protestant denominations to ensure that the language was as inclusive as possible. For example, the assessment was originally called "The Spiritual Growth Indicator." These leaders gave compelling reasons to call it "The Christian Life Profile Assessment."

The Story behind the Christian Life Profile Assessment

This assessment has been through six revisions, including this updated edition. Many people helped along the way, including the staff and congregants of the three churches I have served over the last twenty-five years — Pantego Bible Church, Willow Creek Community Church, and Oak Hills Church. Over the last twenty years, hundreds of churches and organizations have used the assessment and have provided great insights on how to improve it.

The Spiritual State of the Union

The University of Pennsylvania asked The Gallup Organization to help them measure and provide an ongoing benchmark of the "spiritual temperature" in America. One of the indicators chosen was the thirty Key Ideas. For more information on the results and findings, contact The Gallup Organization in Princeton, New Jersey.

The Finished Product

Through my partnership with Zondervan, we have been able to provide the product you now hold in your hands to use in churches, small groups, universities, or organizations. My desire is that you will be able to use this assessment to accomplish the Galatians 4:19 vision in your own life and in the lives of the people you serve: "until Christ is formed in you."

Randy Frazee, San Antonio, Texas

Believe, NIV

Living the Story of the Bible to
Become Like Jesus

Randy Frazee

Grounded in carefully selected Scripture,
Believe, NIV is a unique spiritual growth
experience that takes you on a journey to think,
act, and be more like Jesus. General editor and
pastor Randy Frazee walks you through the ten
key Beliefs of the Christian faith, the ten key Practices of a Jesus-follower,
and the ten key Virtues that characterize someone who is becoming more
like Jesus. Every believer needs to ask these three questions:

- WHAT DO I BELIEVE?

- WHAT SHOULD I DO?

- WHO AM I BECOMING?

Each chapter uses short topical passages from the New International
Version to help you live the story of the Bible. As you journey through this
book, whether in a group or on your own, one simple truth will become
undeniably clear: what you believe drives everything.

Using this edition of *Believe*, church families around the globe can now
embrace a full ministry year through worship services, small group studies,
and family activities. Learn more about this church-wide experience at
BelieveTheStory.com.

Believe Study Guide & DVD

Living the Story of the Bible to Become Like Jesus

Randy Frazee with Randy Larson

The *Believe Study Guide,* designed for use with the *Believe* DVD (sold separately), gives groups of all sizes the opportunity to learn, discuss, and apply what they experience in this 30-session journey through the Bible by exploring 30 essential beliefs, practices, and virtues that every Christian needs to know and live.

Pastor and author Randy Frazee presents 30 ten-minute video teachings on how the story of Scripture helps us think, act, and be like Jesus. You will explore a Key Idea, Key Verse, and application in each session to better understand the 30 essential beliefs, practices and virtues that will help Christians become fully devoted followers of Jesus.

This study guide will guide group members through video discussion for all 30 sessions as well as help individuals grow through in-between-sessions personal study.